NATIONAL
GEOGRAPHIC

In the Tree

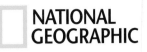

Zoe Sharp

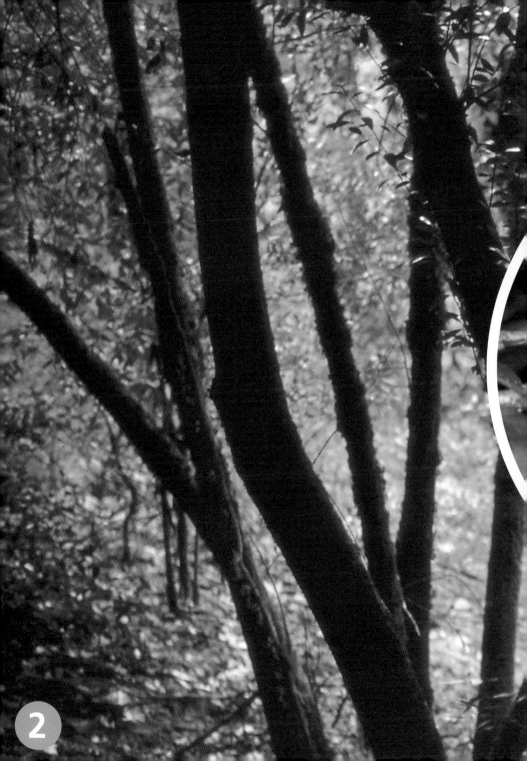

2

Look at me in the tree.

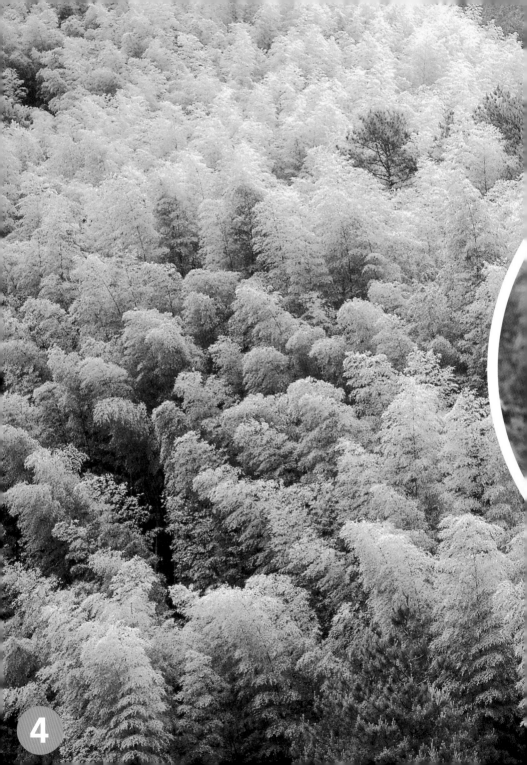

Look at me in the tree.

5

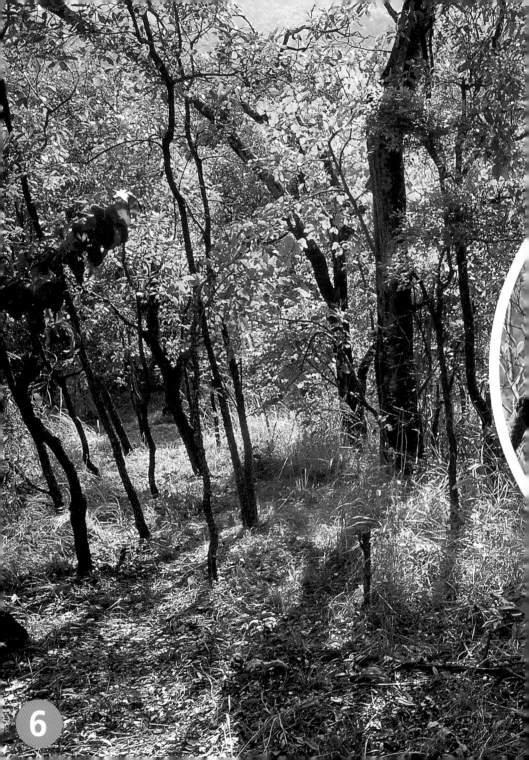

6

Look at me in the tree.

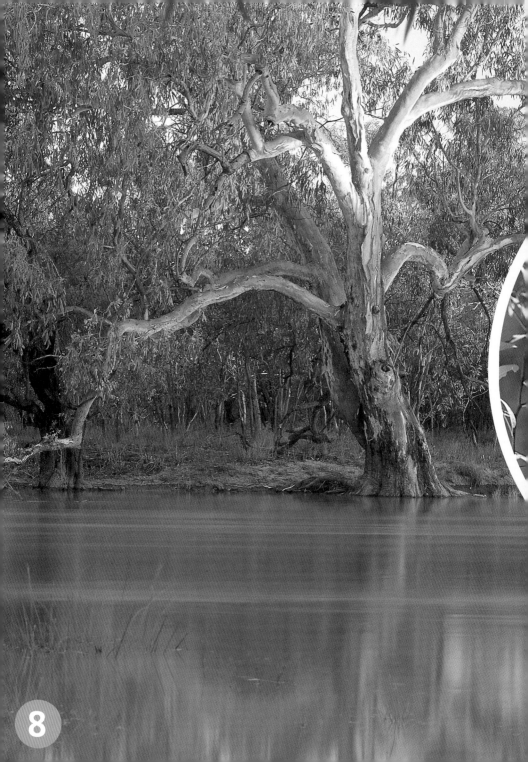

Look at me in the tree.

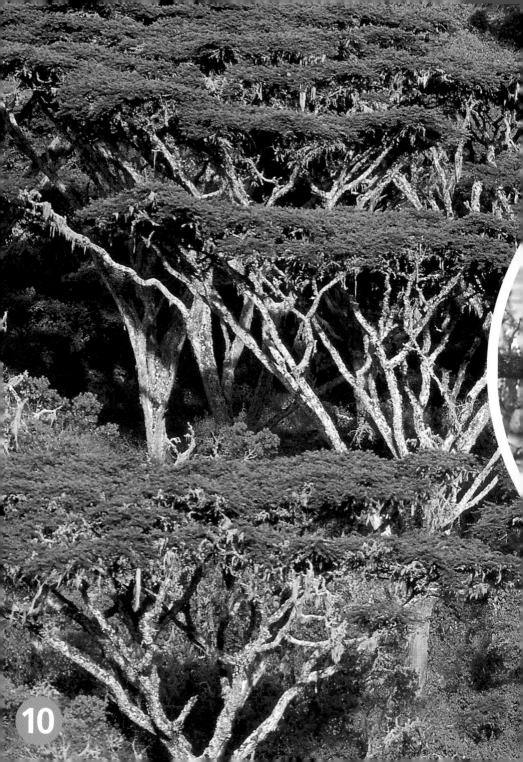

Look at me in the tree.

Look at me in the tree.